LIFE SKILLS

Always Broke?

Skills to Make More Money

Louise Spilsbury

Enslow Publishing
101 W. 23rd Street
Suite 240
New York, NY 10011
USA

enslow.com

Published in 2019 by Enslow Publishing, LLC.
101 W. 23rd Street, Suite 240, New York, NY 10011

Cataloging-in-Publication Data

Names: Spilsbury, Louise.
Title: Always broke? skills to make more money / Louise Spilsbury.
Description: New York : Enslow Publishing, 2019. | Series: Life skills | Includes index.
Identifiers: ISBN 9780766099814 (pbk.) | ISBN 9780766099807 (library bound)
Subjects: LCSH: Finance, Personal--Juvenile literature. | Money--Juvenile literature. | Saving and investment--Juvenile literature. | Financial literacy--Juvenile literature.
Classification: LCC HG179.S65 2019 | DDC 332.024--dc23

Printed in the United States of America

To Our Readers: We have done our best to make sure all website addresses in this book were active and appropriate when we went to press. However, the author and the publisher have no control over and assume no liability for the material available on those websites or on any websites they may link to. Any comments or suggestions can be sent by e-mail to customerservice@enslow.com.

Photo Credits: Cover: Shutterstock: Dobo Kristian; Inside: Shutterstock: Natasa Adzic 44, Andrey Popov 33, Elena Anisimova 9, Roman Babakin 6, Olesia Bilkei 21, Blend Images 5, 39, Serhii Bobyk 4, Caesarstock 7, Diego Cervo 25, Creativa Images 27, Dragon Images 30, Dean Drobot 18, Elenarts 17, Eurobanks 28, Fotos593 34, Goodluz 24, Fer Gregory 42, Antonio Guillem 26, Darrin Henry 41, Holbox 37, Jejim 38, Dmitry Kalinovsky 31, Sergey Kamshylin 11, Dobo Kristian 40, Lightpoet 8, Jacob Lund 19, Alex Makarenko 13, Rob Marmion 14, Melpomene 29, Stuart Miles 35, Photographee.eu 12, Phovoir 20, Joshua Rainey Photography 32, SpeedKingz 43, Armin Staudt 36, Syda Productions 16, 22, Transfuchsian 15, Wavebreakmedia 1, 10, 23, 45.

Contents

Chapter 1
Why Money Matters

Money matters because it helps us to buy, sell, and do things. Money helps us survive, because it allows us to pay for a house or apartment to live in, where we can have shelter. We buy food and drinks with it. It pays for clothes to keep us warm and dry, or to cover us from burning sunshine. Money also buys us many of the things that we do not necessarily need, but which make life fun, such as computers, movie tickets, and games.

Without money we wouldn't be able to pay to do some of the things that we enjoy, such as going to the movies.

Long ago, before people had invented money, they had to exchange things to get the items they needed. This is also called **bartering**. They traded or swapped objects or skills. Bartering still goes on today, in some places and in certain situations. In the past, a pig farmer might trade a pig for some rice from a rice farmer. Today, someone who can fix cars might work on someone else's vehicle in exchange for the car owner fixing their computer.

Money allows us to buy things we need, like food, as well as things we want, like music.

Bartering and exchanging skills and goods can work for a simple **transaction**, but as people want or need more things it gets more complicated. It was not always easy to carry things you want to barter around with you, like potatoes or chickens. It could be tricky to figure out what made a fair trade, and to divide the items. What if you decided a bag of potatoes was only worth half a chicken? Another problem was that food rots, and can be spoiled during transport. Money, in the form of coins, made all this trading much easier. Coins were easy to carry around; you could have different coins worth different amounts, and they kept their value over time.

How Money Is Made

Most countries have two forms of money: coins that are made from metals, and bills that are made from paper. Different countries use different kinds of money, or **currency**. The United Kingdom (UK) uses pounds and pence, for example, while the United States and Canada use dollars and cents. In the United States, there is a range of coins and bills, each worth a different amount.

The main task of the United States Mint is to make sure the people of the nation have enough coins to carry out daily business.

In the United States, paper bills are printed by the US Bureau of Engraving and Printing, and coins are produced by the US Mint. The paper used for this purpose is not like everyday paper, but is rather a mix of cotton and linen. The bills that are used most often, such as the ten dollar bill, may wear out in as little as eighteen months. Bills that get worn out from everyday use are taken out of **circulation** and replaced. Coins last longer because they are made of metal. They usually remain in circulation for about twenty-five years!

Paper money or bills become worn out from everyday use. The US Bureau of Engraving and Printing prints more bills to replace old ones.

THE VALUE OF MONEY

The actual materials from which the money in our wallets and purses is made are not very valuable. Money only has value because everyone agrees that it is worth something. This is very useful when it comes to wages. If you worked for a pig farmer, and all they could pay you with was meat, you would soon get tired of eating pork. You would want to be paid in some other way for all your hard work! That is where money comes in. Money is a measure of the work people do. If someone works seven hours each day, for $12 per hour, their work is worth $84 per day. When wages are paid in money, people can use those coins and bills to pay for all kinds of other things.

It's All About Exchange

Today, few people barter or exchange goods and services directly. We almost always use money instead. Even so, money is still a form of exchange. We exchange money for things we want, like new clothes or tickets to a movie. The money we pay for a single item, like a pair of sneakers, would not pay the wages of the person who designed them. It would not pay the people working in the factory that made the sneakers, or cover the costs of the materials and machines used to make them, or the trucks that transported them to the store. However, when many thousands of people each buy a pair of those sneakers, the money combined becomes a fairer exchange for all the work it took to make them.

We should carefully choose the products we buy with our money.

Money may seem like a boring topic. You may think money is something that should only concern adults, and that you are happy just to get an allowance every week. In fact, money matters to everyone, and understanding money, savings, banks, **credit**, and all the other mysterious things to do with **finance** can help you so much. It can help you to get the things you want now, and in the future. It is also satisfying to feel in control of your own money. Reading this book is a great way to start to learn how to manage your money wisely.

Money stores value, which means that people can save it and then spend it at a later date, when they need something.

Skills for Life

When we have any money, we have to choose how we spend or save it. When we make a choice, we have to give up something else in exchange for the thing that we buy. So when we go to a store to buy a **DVD**, we may have to choose between a comedy or a thriller. If you choose to buy the thriller, you give up the chance to watch the comedy. Once money is gone, it's gone, so make sure you make wise exchanges with yours!

Chapter 2
Earning Money

Most adults have a part-time or full-time job so they can earn money.

Have you ever heard the expression "Money doesn't grow on trees"? It means that money is not easy to come by, and it does not just appear for you to pick it up. Before you can get or spend money, you have to earn it. This is what some people call their wages or **income**. Some people are paid for their work at an hourly rate, so they are paid a certain amount of money for each hour they work. Other people earn a monthly or annual **salary**, a fixed amount of money that covers the hours they are expected to work, or the job they have to complete.

AN ALLOWANCE

Kids are sometimes given money by friends and family as a birthday present or on holidays, and some folks give their kids an allowance. This is a weekly or monthly amount that you can choose to spend or save as you like. Some families give allowances freely, other families ask that the kids earn the money in some way. This could be by washing the car, or raking the yard every week. They get an allowance as a reward for work. That means that if they do not finish the chore they are expected to do, or ask their sibling to do it for them, they do not get the money.

Some kids earn their allowance by helping do chores such as gardening.

BEING RESPONSIBLE FOR YOUR OWN MONEY

Being responsible for your own money is a great thing to learn. Like most things that we earn or are responsible for ourselves, we tend to think more carefully about how we look after it. In other words, if you think someone will just buy you things, you might become really certain that you need that new video game right now! However, if you have to buy it with your own money, you might decide you can live without it, or that you will wait until it comes down in price before purchasing it.

Getting to Work

One day, you will probably need a full-time job to earn a living. To earn money now, you could do some extra chores, or take on a part-time job if you are old enough. Some of the jobs you do as part of a family will probably not be considered work. For example, making your own bed and helping with the laundry are really chores that people perform to do their fair share of household tasks. There are a number of other ways to earn some extra cash. As well as allowing you to earn extra money, these jobs can be great experiences.

Doing some kind of job now will give you valuable experience working with different people. It will also teach you about managing your money, how to earn money, and how to save or spend it as you choose.

Think about the skills you have, and how you could use them to earn money. If you are experienced in helping out in the yard at home, you could offer to weed your neighbors' flower beds, or mow their lawns, in the summer. If you are good with animals, you could offer a dog-walking service, or provide pet care help, such as washing or grooming a dog, or feeding a pet while the owner is on vacation. If you are good with younger children, you could do some babysitting. (You have to be a certain age to babysit, and should be a certified babysitter through the Red Cross.) If you are a musician, you could offer music lessons.

One way to earn extra cash is to walk other people's dogs for them. It can be fun and it is good exercise for you, too.

Before you take on any job, make sure it will not interfere with your school work. Also, make sure you figure out what people will pay you before you start the job, and be willing to **negotiate** your pay. To advertise your availability for work, you could make signs to go in local stores, or make up flyers and leave them at your neighbors' doors. Make sure you have your parent or guardian's permission first!

Making and Selling

A fun way to earn some money is to make and sell things. If you are a good cook, you could have a bake sale. If you are good at crafts, you could make and sell things like scarves or jewelry. If you have a green thumb, you could grow and sell food plants, such as lettuce or herbs, or fresh-cut flowers. You could sell your homemade products from a stand outside your home, or you could think about renting a space at a craft fair.

SELL, SELL, SELL

You can also earn money by selling things you no longer want or need, like games, gadgets, toys, books, or clothes. You can sell items like this by holding a garage sale a couple of times a year, perhaps on a table of your own alongside stuff your parents are selling. It is a great chance to clear out your room. You can also sell unwanted items online through websites like eBay or Craigslist. You might need to ask a parent before you sell something they gave you, or that you own, and you might need their help, especially with selling online.

If you're good at cooking, holding a bake sale is a good way to earn some money.

Skills for Life

How to run a successful bake sale.

- Choose simple but tasty treats to sell. Simple cakes and biscuits are quicker and cheaper to make.

- Ask an adult to go with you to the store and help you buy the ingredients.

- Make sure your hands and all equipment are clean, and ask an adult to help you bake.

- Add up the cost of the ingredients, and figure out how much to sell your items for, so you make a profit.

- Cover a table with a clean, colorful cloth to make your stall look appealing.

- Make a big sign to get people's attention.

- Make sure you have a jar of change in case people pay you with bills.

- Make labels showing the prices for all your items.

- Be polite and friendly to your customers!

Create a large, colorful poster to advertise your bake sale.

15

Chapter 3
The Superpower of Saving

Making and having your own money feels good, but now you have to make choices about what to do with it. Do you spend all your hard-earned cash on movie tickets, or do you save it for something more expensive that you really want?

Before you spend your hard-earned cash, think about whether you'd be better off saving it instead.

SETTING YOUR GOALS

What do you want to save for? If you name your goal, you will reach it faster. It could be a small goal, such as saving for a new app. Or it could be a much bigger goal, like saving for a new bike. Another way of looking at this is in terms of short-term and long-term goals. Saving for a new DVD or app can be achieved in a shorter amount of time. A long-term goal is one that will take you longer to save for, because the item you want to buy is much more expensive, such as a bike or computer. Sometimes, you are not sure what you really want to buy, but you know you want to save, so that you will have money available when you decide what you want.

One reason people save money is that they want to be able to buy a big, expensive item, like a brand new bike.

SAVING YOU FROM MAKING MISTAKES

Saving also helps you avoid making mistakes. When people have their own money, they make choices about what to spend it on. Sometimes, they make a mistake and buy something they never use. That's a waste of money, and if they cannot return the item and get the money back, they have lost the chance to spend that money on something they would really have enjoyed. The smarter financial decision is to save some of your money. That way you get time to think carefully about what you really want to spend it on. Then you are less likely to make a mistake, and less likely to waste your hard-earned cash.

Balancing Budgets

A **budget** is a plan that balances the money a person has coming in—their income—with the money going out. The money people need to spend is called their **expenses**. Many adults make a budget every month or every year. They figure out how much money they earn from their job, and how much money they spend on things like rent, groceries, utilities such as electricity and water, and **payments** on a house or car, for example. Once they know exactly what must be spent on these essentials, they can figure out what will be left over. That is the money available for less necessary things, such as new clothes, a vacation, or decorating the home.

A budget is a way of adding up all the money you expect to come in, and planning what needs to be spent and what you would like to spend.

MAKE YOUR OWN BUDGET

To make a budget, first add up all of your income, including any money you earn from working, your allowance, and birthday or holiday gifts. That is the amount of money you have to spend or save. Next, add up all your expenses. This is the money you plan to spend on the things you need or want. Think carefully about this. Ask yourself if you really need an item, or just really want it. There may be many things you would like to buy, but realistically none of us can have everything we want, so try to prioritize.

HOW TO BALANCE A BUDGET

Once you have figured out how much you absolutely need to spend, you are left with an amount to spend how you choose. To balance your budget, you now need to decide how much of that money to spend or save. For example, you could save 50 percent of it, spend 40 percent of it immediately, and perhaps **donate** 10 percent of it to a **charity** of your choice. The way you divide up your budget is entirely up to you. You could put the money into three separate jars, boxes, or wallets. Then any time you make money by doing chores or receiving birthday gifts, you can divide it between the containers.

You could leave enough in your spending budget to afford outings with your friends.

Make It Happen

People who set themselves a savings goal generally save faster than those who do not, but saving can still be hard. Even if you really want to save up for that bike, cell phone, or computer, there may be times when you are tempted to spend your money instead. There are lots of ways to help make saving happen. Tell your family and friends what you are saving for. This makes it real, and makes you more determined. Be firm. If you tell yourself that the money you are trying to save every month is something you really must do, you are less likely to let it slide.

Telling other people what you are saving for means they can help by encouraging you to stick to your plan and reach your goal.

DOING THINGS FOR FREE

Another way to make saving easier is to find free things to have and do. For example, when you are heading out for a game in the park with your friends, take a bottle of water with you so you do not have to buy a soda when you're thirsty. Instead of going to the movies with your friends, invite them to your house to watch a DVD, and make pizzas rather than buying them. Think about all the fun you can have for free.

Skills for Life

To help you save for more expensive items, it can help to create a savings plan or chart. First, find out the cost of the things you want. Then figure out how long it will take you to save for them by dividing the amount you need to save by the weekly amount you earn. Make a chart to show the number of weeks you need to save, and use some kind of **graphic**, like a jar filling up, with different levels for each week. Color in each level as you fill up your fund. This will help you to feel you are getting closer to your goal.

There are lots of things you can do for fun for free to help you save money, like hanging out with your friends.

Chapter 4
All About Banks

Some people put their saved-up dollars and cents in a jar. Others put it under the mattress of their bed. The trouble with keeping savings at home is that there is always the temptation to dip into the money to buy little things, rather than sticking to the plan to save it. Money can become lost in your room, too! That is why your parents or caregivers might suggest you put your money in a bank, instead. You have probably seen banks in your local neighborhood, or been in one with your family. There are also banks that people use online. People put their money in these banks to keep it safe when they are not using it.

It's good to keep your money in a bank because a bank keeps it safe and makes it easier for you to save.

MONEY IN, MONEY OUT

When people put their money in a bank, we say they are making a **deposit** of money. You can deposit money in different ways. You can hand it over to a worker in a bank branch or put it in an envelope and insert it into an ATM. In the bank, deposits are put into a big, secure safe. This is an incredibly strong, locked cabinet or room. Your money is safe in it until you need to take some out. When you take money out of a bank, you make a **withdrawal**.

ACCOUNTS

If you want to use a bank, you need to open an **account** there. To do this, your parent gives details to the bank such as your name, address, and date of birth, and something to prove who you are, such as a birth certificate. The bank then opens an account in your name. It has a unique number that you should keep a record of. The bank records exactly how much money you have in your account, after your deposits and withdrawals. You can check how much is in your account at any time online at your bank's website, or at an ATM, or at the bank.

It is easy to get cash from your bank account when you need it, day or night, from an ATM.

How Banks Work

Banks are businesses and, like other businesses, they need to make money. They do this partly by giving it away! Banks do not only keep your money safe, they also pay you some extra money for doing so. The little bit of money they pay you is called **interest**. Interest is a **percentage**, or portion, of how much money you keep with them. The amount of interest added to the total in your account will fall if you make a withdrawal from the account, but it will rise again as you add more.

Setting up a bank account can help you save money for the future.

INTEREST-ING CALCULATIONS

Say you deposit $100 in your account, and the interest rate is 2 percent per year. That means the bank adds $2 of interest to your account each year. It is not much, but if you have $1,000, over one year the interest is $20. If you keep the money in the account the next year, then further interest builds on the $1,020. Over many years, you may have earned hundreds more dollars in interest just by doing nothing!

LOANING MONEY

The reason banks can pay out interest is that they earn even more money by loaning your money to other people. People go to banks to borrow money to buy expensive things, such as houses and cars. It would take many years from most people's salaries or wages to save the money needed to buy such things, and often people do not want to wait that long! All the money in a bank's customers' savings accounts adds up to a sizeable amount that the bank can loan. Banks agree to loan money on the condition that people pay it back over an agreed length of time, and pay interest on the amount they borrowed. Sometimes, to make even more money in interest payments, banks loan even more money than they actually hold from their customers. They are certain they will make enough in interest payments to cover the difference.

Banks loan money to people who want to start up their own businesses.

Choosing an Account

Banks have different types of accounts available. A **checking account** is for money that you use to pay for regular things like rent, bills, or groceries. Instead of using cash to pay large bills, people can write a **check** or pay with a **debit card**. A debit card is a plastic card used to transfer money electronically from one account to another. Usually, adults with homes, families, or businesses have these accounts. You sometimes pay a small fee to have a checking account. If you are saving money, you should choose a **savings account** because you will get more interest in a savings account than a checking account. Banks usually offer several savings accounts, with different rates of interest.

When you have a bank account you can get a debit card that allows you to pay for things from online stores.

Interest rate: Obviously, the higher the interest rate the better! However, interest rates may be highest on accounts where you leave the money for longer without taking any out. Banks sometimes change their interest rates, so check regularly that you are still getting the most interest you can.

Savings amount: Some savings accounts may only be available to people who make large regular deposits, or deposit a large initial sum.

Fees: Avoid savings accounts which charge monthly fees to manage your money. This eats away at the interest earned.

Different accounts offer different rates of interest, so research which account is best for you before making your choice.

Skills for Life

Your bank account can help you earn money over time while keeping your money safe. Choosing the wrong account can waste your money, or its potential to earn interest. So always ask a parent or other caregiver to help you choose the best savings account, and get their permission to open any account. Keep a notebook with details of all your deposits and withdrawals. Regularly compare this to your bank balance, to make sure the account total is correct, because banks sometimes make mistakes! Also, get an adult to help you make sure any interest has been added correctly.

Have you ever borrowed some money from a parent or other caregiver to buy something that costs more than the amount you have saved? If so, then you have used credit. Credit means borrowing money and promising to pay it back. Of course, you would pay back your parent or caregiver, when you next have some money coming in. If you are lucky, they will not charge you interest on their loan. Banks, however, do charge interest on credit, because that is how they make money.

Some people borrow money from a bank to buy their first car. This is one way of using credit.

TYPES OF CREDIT

Credit is often in the form of a loan. For example, borrowing money to buy a car is a way of using credit. Borrowers usually pay back the loan in small, regular amounts that they can afford. The other common form of credit is a **credit card** from a bank. Using one of these plastic cards to pay for something means the bank is lending you the money to pay for it. It will not lend any amount, but instead sets a top limit. Not surprisingly, this is called your credit limit.

It's important to pay back a loan or you could end up with a bad credit score that will affect your chances of getting credit in the future.

A MATTER OF TRUST

Credit is all about trust. If you have borrowed money from a family member before, and not paid it back, they might think twice about lending money to you again. People need to earn trust to get credit. Everyone who wants a loan, or other form of credit, is checked for their credit score. This is a measure of how well someone has performed using credit in the past. For example, it includes information on whether someone has ever repaid part of a loan late, whether they are already using credit, or have spent more money than their bank account has in it. If there are too many of these mistakes, or factors affecting a person's ability to repay a loan, their credit score will be lower and it will be more difficult for them to get new credit.

How Credit Cards Work

Credit cards seem amazing. Just by presenting a piece of plastic, adults can buy all sorts of things without handing over any money. That is how it seems, but in reality credit cards do not use free money. They are borrowing money, and that money must be repaid, with interest, each month.

Credit cards are a useful way to spend, but only if you can pay back the bank quickly, otherwise the interest on your purchases grows over time.

PAYBACK TIME

Imagine you desperately want a $300 drone to play with, and your parent or caregiver buys it on a credit card. This is what happens: at the end of the month, the person with the credit card account gets a statement from the bank showing they have spent $300 on their card. To help pay for the service of providing credit, the bank requests a minimum payment. This is the lowest amount the account holder needs to pay. However, it is best to pay off more than the minimum payment each month, because of the interest rate. A credit card account's interest rate is its **annual percentage rate**, or APR. This is often around 20 percent. That means that if the person paid off none of the loan during a year, they would need to pay 20 percent interest on the $300, on top of the $300 itself. That is $60, making the total cost of the drone $360. That drone is suddenly more expensive!

The trouble with credit cards is that more interest is added each month. If only a minimum payment is made one month, the total spending on the card, less that payment, is carried over to the next month. This gets added to new purchase amounts during the next month, and the interest on the new total grows. When people pay more than the minimum amount each month, they pay back the loan more quickly, with less interest. Repaying a loan in four months rather than twelve could drop the overall borrowing cost.

Credit cards can be used to buy things we want, but we need to be able to pay off that debt quite quickly or the interest will add up.

The Deal With Debt

Debt is money that you owe. Some debt can be useful, such as money borrowed to buy a home to live in, or to pay the fees that put a student through college. This is an **investment** of money for the future. That is because property often increases in value over time, and college study can help students find better paid jobs. The future worth of these things is often greater than what people actually pay for them. What is more, the interest rates on these loans can be fairly low.

*People may become homeless if they are unable to meet **mortgage** and rent debts.*

BAD DEBT

Other types of debt, however, are bad. People build up bad debt when they buy things that quickly lose their value using loans or credit cards that charge very high interest. Some people get to the stage where they can only pay off their existing debts by taking out more and more loans. Some cash loans have interest rates as high as 300 percent a year. This means paying $300 to borrow $100! People can even end up repaying more in interest than the original amount of the loan itself. The burden of bad debt can bring misery to families and individuals.

Loans can lead to debt, and debt hangs on long after the thrill of a new purchase is over...

Skills for Life

If you ever get money troubles from debt, there are two main steps to take to help you get out of trouble.

1 **Budget:** Make a list of what you spent last month. How much of that money did you not need to spend, such as on treats? Next month use this money to pay off your debt.

2 **Rank your debts:** Make a list of all the debts you have, ordered by the amount of interest charged. Pay off the highest interest loans first, such as credit cards, and the minimum on the lowest interest loans. Once the worst debt source is paid off, move to the next one down the list.

Chapter 6
Spend, Spend, Spend?

To be able to manage money well, it is important to sort out the difference between what we need and what we want. Have you ever heard yourself saying things like, "I just have to have that new cell phone," or, "I need to buy that video game today"? Do you really need those things? Needs are things that we cannot do without. You need a toothbrush, food, school clothes, and equipment such as pens to use for schoolwork. The things we want, but do not necessarily need, are items such as magazines and movies. It is good to work on figuring out the difference.

There's a difference between spending money on what we need, like a toothbrush and toothpaste, and buying what we want.

FIGURE IT OUT

What we need and what we want may not always be clear cut. We need food to survive, but what we really need is foods such as **protein**, **carbohydrates**, fruits, and vegetables to get the **nutrients** and energy that keep us healthy. Ice cream, chips, and soda are food and drink, but we do not need them! Sometimes you have to spend money on something that you need immediately, such as lunch, or a new tire for your bike. Other times, when we are thinking of buying something we want, it is good to take a minute. Think about whether it is really worth buying that game, or comic, or candy.

Think about purchases carefully. If you drink a cool, refreshing glass of water instead of buying a soda, you'd save money. Water is much better for your teeth, too.

DON'T WASTE IT

Before you buy, think about how much money you have now, how much you will need later in the month, and whether you really need or want the item. Money is a precious thing that you or your parents have worked for. Buy what you can afford. It is much better to have money in the bank than a bedroom full of stuff you don't use much and no cash. Just do the math! For example, if you spend $3 every week on soda, after a year you will have spent $156. That could have bought you a big or truly useful purchase.

Smart Shopping

When you have spent your money, it's gone. It makes sense to shop wisely, to make sure you get the most out of your money. When you see something you want or need, it makes sense not to buy it immediately. Make a note of the price one store is charging, and then shop around. Check the price of your item in other stores, and check online, too.

BE THRIFTY

Being money smart means making sure you shop around and don't spend more than you need to— you might find just the right outfit for you in a thrift store, for example.

Often, people buy a new item when really a used or preowned one would be cheaper and just as good. For example, if you want to buy a book that you know you will read only once, consider buying it from a thrift store, where it will be much cheaper. You could even pass it back to the thrift store when you're done with it. Finding vintage clothes in a thrift store is not only great fun, it's also a great way to create a totally individual style.

GIVING GIFTS

Giving gifts to people we care about feels great. We want to give loved ones something they will really like, but you can still shop wisely. During the holiday season, for example, you could make a list of who you want to get a gift for, and figure out how much you can afford to spend on everyone, before you start buying anything. That way you will avoid running out of cash before you have all your gifts. Also consider giving gifts that you have made, as these can cost very little. You could bake cookies, create a piece of art, make a necklace, or knit a scarf. You could give parents tokens they can trade in for a back-rub or a car wash. Think outside the box!

Making homemade gifts for people costs less, is fun to do, and will be greatly appreciated by the recipient.

Make Your Own Choices

Advertisements are all around us: on TV, YouTube, apps, billboards, magazines, newspapers, movies, the internet, social media, and more. Advertisements use lots of different tactics, images, and catchy tunes to make us aware of a product and to persuade us to buy it. Some ads try to make you buy something you didn't even know you wanted, or knew existed! Ads are not there to inform us. They are there to sell us things! Being aware of this, and the way ads work, will help you to make your own choices!

Advertisements are all around us, trying to persuade us we need the latest products, but do we really?

UNDERSTANDING ADVERTISEMENTS

It is important to be able to look at or hear advertisements critically and to be aware that advertisers always try to make their products look good or better than they really are. Some use famous movie or sports stars to promote their product. Some suggest that you will seem more grown-up if you use their product, or that your parents are great parents if they give you the product! Some advertisements try to sell more products by giving away something for free, like a toy in a box of cereal.

Don't be persuaded by friends or peer pressure to buy something you don't need or want.

PEER PRESSURE

There is another kind of pressure that may make us want to buy more stuff, and that is peer pressure. Peer pressure is when friends or people of the same age make us want to do something. Think about the items in your bedroom. Ask yourself why you wanted each one, and how often you have used it. Did you get or ask for some things just because your friends had them? When you want something new, think carefully to figure out whether you want it just because people you know have it, or if you really, truly like it and want it yourself.

Keeping Track

Money matters can get complicated. You may have definite goals for saving money to buy expensive things, spending needs each week or month, wish lists of things you might like to buy some day if you have any money left over, and unexpected expenses such as a new baseball glove to replace a broken one. Then you have the added uncertainty of how much interest you are getting on your savings, or paying out if you have loans. Often your bank account records will help you to keep track of your money. A good way to feel in better control of your money, however, is to keep your own records in a notebook.

Keeping track of your money will give you more to spend in the long run.

CASH FLOW JOURNAL

A cash flow journal is simply a chart with columns to fill in. The simplest sort has one column headed "Date," one headed "Deposits," one headed "Withdrawals," and one headed "Balance." At the start of each month, write the starting balance, which is how much money you have in your account. Then in rows write the date and fill in the amounts in each column as necessary. Adjust the balance on each date by subtracting or adding these amounts from or to it. You can also do a more complicated version, with columns for categories of spending, such as food, clothes, leisure activities, and savings, and have a row for every day of the month.

Skills for Life

You can use your budget tracking to help make decisions about whether you need or just want to buy things:

Want or Need

Want

Do you already have anything that does the same job that you can make do with?

Yes → Don't buy

No → Can you pay for it from your budget?

Yes → Buy

No → Start saving

Need

Can you pay for it from your budget?

Yes → Buy

No → Can it wait until after you have gotten your allowance or been paid?

Yes → Buy next month

No → Buy using savings

You could keep track of your cash flow on your computer or in a notebook.

41

Be a Thoughtful Consumer

Waste, and how we choose to handle it, affects our world's **environment**. Waste is anything we throw away or get rid of that does not get used. Waste can cause **pollution**, and burying it in **landfills** uses up valuable land that people need. When people demand more and more things, companies use more energy and materials to make them, and this contributes to pollution and to **global warming**, too. We can all make a difference by becoming thoughtful consumers. That means reducing the amount we buy, and creating less waste. This means we can save money and save the planet at the same time!

REDUCE

We can reduce the amount we buy by considering our purchases more carefully. We can also reduce the amount of packaging we buy. For example, plastic packaging is made from oil, and making and disposing of plastics releases polluting gases into the air. You could make your own sandwiches and put them in a reusable container, rather than buying shrink-wrapped sandwiches in a store.

Making your own lunch and carrying it in recyclable or reusable packaging saves you money and is good for the environment too.

REUSE

There are lots of ways to reuse things. You can repair clothes that have a slight rip or have lost a button rather than throwing them away and buying new ones. You can cover a hole with a fun patch, or adapt old clothes to make them wearable, such as cutting off old jeans to make a cool pair of shorts.

Recycling stuff rather than throwing it all in the trash is easy to do and makes you a thoughtful consumer.

RECYCLE

Many products like cans, bottles, paper, and cardboard can be remade into either the same kind of thing or new products. Making new items from recycled ones uses less energy and fewer resources than making things from new materials. For example, a recycled plastic soda bottle can be turned into combs, computer cases, and many other kinds of plastic products. Ask your local recycling office about what can be recycled, and start collecting recyclable items now.

Make the Most of Your Money

There are lots of things money just cannot buy, like a sunny day that makes you smile, or good friends. These things make us really happy. Although you might get a temporary buzz from buying the latest game or some trendy jeans, these things won't really make you any happier. Money is important and useful, however, because it can pay for the things we need and make our lives more comfortable, and we can use it to buy experiences and other things that give our families and friends some fun. Managing your money well will allow you to use more of it for the things that really matter, and give you a well-deserved feeling of self-confidence and pride.

Store sale signs are designed to tempt you to spend, but think about whether you really need an item before you buy it.

THE POWER TO DO GOOD

Money does have the power to do a lot of good. You can donate money in a collection, or give some to your favorite charities. Some charities allow you to choose to buy books, a goat, some chickens, or a range of other useful, life-changing gifts for a struggling family in another country. Some charities help particular groups of people, for example, people needing a medical procedure. Other charities use donated money to help animals, from caring for orphaned elephants to funding wildlife reserves. There is sure to be a charity that matches your interests.

Skills for Life

There is one last golden rule to take away with you: the "sleep-on-it-for-twenty-four-hours" rule. When you are shopping, it is easy to get excited about making a purchase, especially if the store has signs up saying there is a sale on, or that suggest the item is selling fast. The trick is to wait at least twenty-four hours, or overnight, before you commit to that purchase. The idea is that if you wait and think it over, you will be better able to decide if you really do want or need that item.

There are a lot of charities to choose from, so you could find a charity in a particular area of interest of yours and donate to that.

Glossary

account An arrangement with a bank to hold your money and keep records of transactions.

annual percentage rate The yearly rate charged for borrowing, or earned through an investment.

bartering Exchanging goods or services for other goods or services without using money.

budget A plan for spending your money that balances your income with what you need to spend.

carbohydrates Foods such as pasta or rice that provide the body with energy.

charity An organization that helps people or animals in need, or parts of the environment, such as rainforests.

check A piece of paper that instructs the bank to make a payment from your account.

checking account A bank account which pays little or no interest, but from which the customer can withdraw money whenever he or she wants.

circulation The availability of something to the public.

credit An arrangement to receive money from a bank or products from a store, and pay for it later.

credit card A plastic card issued by a bank and used to buy items with borrowed money.

currency A system of money in use in a particular country, such as dollars and cents.

debit card A card allowing the holder to transfer money electronically from their bank account when making a purchase.

debt Money that you owe.

deposit A sum of money paid into a bank.

donate To give money to a good cause such as a charity.

environment The natural world, the air, water, and land around us.

expenses Money people need to spend, on things such as food and bills.

finance To do with money.

global warming The increase in Earth's temperature that most scientists agree is caused by an increase in polluting gases in the air.

graphic A clear and effective picture.

income Money that is earned from doing work or received from investments or business.

interest Money paid regularly at a particular rate for the use of money loaned.

investment Putting money into something such as a business to make a profit from it later.

landfills Places where waste is buried in large, deep pits.

mortgage A big bank loan people take out to buy a property.

negotiate To discuss something in order to come to a deal over it.

nutrients Substances in food that keep us healthy.

payments Small amounts of money, usually due monthly, that add up over time to pay back large loans.

percentage A rate or proportion per hundred.

pollution Something which dirties or poisons a part of the environment.

protein Substance found in foods such as meat, eggs, and nuts that the body needs to be healthy.

salary An amount of money earned every month or year, for work done.

savings account A bank account that earns interest on money saved.

transaction The action of buying or selling something.

withdrawal The action of taking money out of a bank account.

Further Reading

BOOKS

Karlitz, Gail and Debbie Honig. *Growing Money: A Complete Investing Guide for Kids.* New York: Price Stern Sloan, 2010.

McGillian, Jamie Kyle. *The Kids' Money Book: Earning, Saving, Spending, Investing, Donating.* New York: Sterling Children's Books, 2016.

McKenna, James, Jeannine Glista and Matt Fontaine. *How to Turn $100 into $1,000,000: Earn! Save! Invest!* New York: Workman Publishing, 2016.

Toren, Adam and Matthew. *Kidpreneurs: Young Entrepreneurs With Big Ideas!* Phoenix, AZ: Business Plus Media, 2016.

WEBSITES

The Mint
www.themint.org
Find out more about ways to earn money.

Rich Kid Smart Kid
www.richkidsmartkid.com
Play some games that help you be smart with your money.

Ducksters
http://www.ducksters.com/money/how_money_is_made_bills.php
Take a field trip to the money factory!

Index